Politics and Pandemics

poems by

Milton Jordan

Finishing Line Press
Georgetown, Kentucky

Politics and Pandemics

I wonder what instruments are playing
And are they dancing; or gazing at the earth?
Ed Dorn, Collected Poems 1956-1974
Four Seasons Press, 1975

Copyright © 2022 by Milton Jordan
ISBN 978-1-64662-838-4 First Edition
All rights reserved under International and Pan-American Copyright Conventions. No part of this book may be reproduced in any manner whatsoever without written permission from the publisher, except in the case of brief quotations embodied in critical articles and reviews.

ACKNOWLEDGMENTS

Many of these poems, or earlier versions of them, have appeared in the following anthologies, online and print journals, blogs and email blasts:

The Texas Poetry Calendar; "This Week," a now & then email blast
The Ethicist: Interfaith Stories Inaugural Issue
San Antonio Express News; the anthology *No Season for Silence: Texas Poets and Pandemic,* Kallisto Gaia Press, 2020
The Racket, an online journal
Spitball, *Lily Poetry Review*
the chapbook, *Better Things to Do,* Bottom Dog Press
The Ocotillo Review, the anthology *Odes and Elegies: Eco Poetry from the Texas Gulf Coast,* Lamar Literary Press, 2020
Good Cop/Bad Cop: An Anthology, Flowersong Press, 2021
Arts Alive, San Antonio
Texas Poetry Assignment

Publisher: Leah Huete de Maines

Editor: Christen Kincaid

Cover Art: Backed by area clergy and faith leaders, Rabbi Neil Blumofe addresses the press and supporters of the Texas Impact "Faith for Fair Elections" Lobby Day. Photo by Bee Moorhead courtesy of Texas Impact.

Author Photo: Anne Elton Jordan

Cover Design: Elizabeth Maines McCleavy

Order online: www.finishinglinepress.com
also available on amazon.com

Author inquiries and mail orders:
Finishing Line Press
PO Box 1626
Georgetown, Kentucky 40324
USA

Table of Contents

Blinded by the Corona 1
My Hands and I 2
A Fracking Disaster 3
Permian Dreams 4
Politics and Pandemic 5
Leadership in Crisis 6
Maintaining Law and Order 7
Live P D 8
In Praise of a Persistent Generation 9
Greenwood in Flames 10
One July Night in Portland 11
Beyond the Wall 12
Bordering on Lines from Neruda 13
Cross Cultural Dialogue 14
That Tragic Border 15
Once a Union Maid 16
Neglecting Repair 17
Remembering 18
Garden Lessons 19
When We Celebrated This Season 20
Grandfather's Monologues 21
Remembered Highways 22
Recollections 23
Somewhat Independent Living 24
Delaying a Gift 25
Watching Swallows 26
The Realization 27
Creation's Lament 28
Distanced Ritual 29
The Feast in a Strict Season 30
Calculating the Damage 31
No Season for Silence 32
A Grammar of Good Trouble 33
In the Beginning 34

Blinded by the Corona

The decade began on a widespread scare
(if counting begins at zero).
Here in the great state we demanded,
as is our wont, someone to blame,
Chinese or some other strangers,
perhaps some politician we dislike.
We yearn for new headlines and talking heads
proclaiming replacement crises, turning
our attention to other concerns
or, please Lord, the lack of one.

My Hands and I

Today I find myself staring again
at my own hands, palms up in my lap,
wondering what will become of these
instruments, which once gripped other
tools and put them to forgotten use,
now laid aside, stored as those other tools
replaced by more efficient technologies?

We've cornered the market on idleness
not knowing if new tasks might appear
or if the muscle will remember
forgotten skills or develop those
required for something to put us to use.

A Fracking Disaster

Just enough breeze to ruffle dust across
our drought bare yard under glaring sunlight
could not ease mid-morning heat nor painful
afternoon fieldwork with little promise
of crops worth any effort to harvest.
We surrendered green grass lawns five years
before increasing water use restriction
closed another field your great-grandfather
homesteaded ninety-six years ago.

Each August our once plentiful river
runs, if at all, in rivulets past sand bars
and dry red dirt islands without growth.
Upstream drilling rigs demand acre feet
daily to pump underground cracking shale
then out again to stagnant polluted pools,

In air-conditioned chambers the governor
and legislature grant another permit
with laws that prohibit local action
that might interfere with the industry.

Permian Dreams

Nearly as invisible as methane
spewing skyward from abandoned well sites
corporate executives eased away
from leased office spaces under cover
of shelter in place pandemic practices
to cash their bonus checks at distant banks
while lawyers filed bankruptcy protection plans.
Owners of new office buildings and luxury
condo rentals holding their own leases
stared at stacks of paper worth pennies a page
and in Hobbs and Eunice, Kermit and Andrews
dreams seeped away silently as toxic
fluids in fields with their own bankruptcies.

Politics and Pandemics

Flummoxed and fulminating, trapped in
now discredited denial and missing
leadership politicians proclaim relief
but abdicate authority and dispense
dangerous advice and nasty slogans,
closing often with questionable calls
for prayer, while bars open as quickly
as new virus cases are announced
and growing numbers of vulnerable
citizens wait for some hopeful word
of policies or plans aimed at more
than a politician's self-protection.

Leadership in Crisis

Running fully three months ahead of good sense
our over anxious governor relaxed
stay home, stay safe rules he'd been three weeks late
declaring as the virus began to spread.
Business reopened, masks disappeared
and the governor's supporters acclaimed
increased business activity across
the state well worth the increase in cases
reported in every urban area.

Maintaining Law and Order

Two deputies drove their well-marked county
sheriff's van slowly onto the cracked
asphalt lot near the old gym behind Strong
Middle School where lines of people stood
in circles drawn for social distance
waiting for the Salvation Army's free
distribution of fifty pound boxes
of produce donated by city merchants.

Half the crowd quickly abandoned their places
and disappeared across the grass playground,
to retrieve their pick-ups in safer times
while the deputies laughed at the repeated
success of this experiment they'd tried
before on the other side of town.

Live P. D.

Martin L. K. Johnson, Booker Bonham,
Javier Suarez and Pete Valenzuela
wearing baggy, drawstring denim trousers
over union suits fading to grey
and cheap plastic flip flops, standard issue
for a sheriff's department inmate,
stand three afternoon vigil hours along
the drive dropping to basement holding cells
beneath the new county office building,
three Saturday evening hours marking
the time their fifth crew member, Julian
had before the hearse brought him up that drive.

In Praise of
A Persistent Generation

> *When the woods are full of police*
> *You cannot write poems about trees.*
> Bertolt Brecht, 1943

Shall you write of your city streets when you
must avoid patrols on every corner?
Shall you sing of your sidewalks if dancing
will lead to your arrest and your vision
blurs in another choking gas fog?
You don't stop along highways to Houston
where sheriff's deputies haunt every roadhouse
and rest area designed for others.

Nevertheless you sing aloud and dance
to imagined tunes you remember
with guitar strings and friendly voices
sounding forth from balconies and doorways.
Your singing's more threatening than slinging stones,
your dancing more persistent than tear gas.

Greenwood in Flames: Tulsa, 1921 - 2020

At that place where white violence destroyed
black lives and businesses a century before
Make America White Again rallied
as pandemic threats spread out across
states and cities reopening without caution.
Unmasked and crowded well short of social
distance, the mob declaimed in word and deed
disdain for lives they deemed expendable.

One July Night in Portland

We can, perhaps, credit Donavan's name
to some 1960s pop rock star,
but credit for the less lethal missile
fracturing his skull belongs to federal
marshalls who "fired only low impact rounds."
We can neither name nor hold to account
the camouflaged crew, unidentified,
pushing others into unmarked vans,
but we can credit unnecessary
occupations to the punitive
policy maker buying bragging rights.

Beyond the Wall

> *When they say they're praying about their decision,*
> *they've already decided.*
>   Mark Jarman, "Don't Get Your Hopes Up."

Not that my camel could not thread the needle's eye
but every needle within my reach eyeless.
No matter the sharpest point, every project
I imagined aborted before it began.
Cloth, plain or patterned, in my hands showed no stitch,
no mending nor decorative borders,
and leaders I petitioned for useful tools
answered with prayerful words but empty hands,
narrowed eyes watching from inside the city's gate.

Bordering on Lines from Neruda

Man kills it with paper and with hate,
smothers it in a rug of the everyday, shreds it
among the hostile barbed-wire clothes. *

We choose in this strict and tensioned season
to clothe our housekeepers and fruit pickers
in undergarments woven of barbed wire.
Discomfort you know discourages planning
and conversation beyond pained complaint.

We excuse this unofficial, well-hidden practice
with celebrations of patriotic virtue
and the essential demands of law and order
often proclaiming our compassion for all
and demanding others respect their freedom.

- From *The Heights of Macchu Picchu*, section 2 in the translation by David Young.

Cross Cultural Dialogue

Did you sit, Honduran, among the rocks
above the muddy boundary river and watch,
beyond its meager flow, the grandsons
of paramilitary trainers who taught
those who patrolled your neighborhoods
and claimed the crops of your father's parents?

Do you hear me answer in my untrained Spanish
or does your norte ear notice no such sound?
Why are your crews along the bank armed
with equipment for careful calculation
lining out the track for paneled walls that speak
only the violent language of keep out?

That Tragic Border

Did her mother see the image of Valeria
facedown in the river's shallows still clinging
to her father's neck lying lifeless beside her?

Hidden in her home in El Salvador
did she recognize her daughter's delicate arm
draped over Oscar's once stronger shoulder?
What promised future must she now reimagine?

When these best hopes die do Salvadoran mothers
come forth from fear and hiding spitting fury
at local gangs and distant politicians
who plot their own selfish futures
without regard for mothers or their hopes?

Once a Union Maid

Restraining her movement hurled her words
across the room as he stood in his door
to the secretarial pool. She walked
past three others staring wide eyed
as she spoke: "Can you see that clock, Mister,
hanging above the door beyond our desks?
We do not have time to correct your mistakes
and get your letter in the outgoing mail."

She took the letter from his hand to her desk,
picked up her purse and walked out the door.
Others pulled purses from hiding places
and smiling followed her out ten minutes
before Friday's five o'clock quitting time.

Neglecting Repair

> *I'm sorry, my son, but you're too late in asking*
> *Mr. Peabody's coal train has hauled it away.*
> John Prine

Now our grandchildren are left to dismantle
twisted and destructive systems we've built
from want and excess and careless disregard
for one another and the futures
we had assumed to be assured.

These children may wonder at the failure
of their parents to recalibrate
ledgers with strangely unequal columns
or to reconstruct bare broken hillsides,
but you and I will be held to account
for neglected meadows and forgotten
neighbors who kept our twisted systems turning.

Remembering

Late morning shadows lying like leaves along
roots just west of bare limbed trees marking
the sunrise side of our small settlement
of mostly empty unplumbed houses where
workers were kept through each season's harvest.
Remembering frames these online photos,
in less than living color, of two charred
trunks left standing beyond ash dusted
debris, the shell of one four room house.

Garden Lessons

Tomorrow you will learn the language
of dirt, the inflections of growing things,
what each stalk drains up out of the earth
as its tropic climb reaches toward the sun
turning one direction then another,
flexible in its strength, bending with wind
and stretching away from every comfort
of lifelessness, reaching each day above
itself and depending on nothing
but desire and dissatisfaction,
and that creative tugging toward the sun.

When We Celebrated This Season

Every zephyr drifting off the prairie
over this town built where hills begin
to rise into more rugged country
disturbs post oak and mesquite, the litter
left when crowds went home for drinks or supper.

Three of us arrested Friday night
for drunk and disorderly sweep the walks
shoveling dung dropped behind the sheriff's
Citizens Mounted Posse following
the parade we watched from barred windows.

Others who avoided arrest watch now
through plate glass fronting Booker's Brew
And Barbecue, knowing our release
comes Sunday when the bars are closed.

Grandfather's Monologues

Our children say their children have heard
and understood experts explaining
intricate calculations required
for sending satellites to predetermined
points in galaxies across light years.
Can we describe scenes to interest them
when they have seen full color images
of the surfaces of distant planets
snapped by robots controlled from Houston?

Will the tedium of oft repeated
stories hold their attention beyond
our description of rivers merging
before the Bureau built their high dam?
Tales of now well known forests once dark
and dense with forbidding undergrowth
no longer entertain children whose hands
hold the latest virtual gaming devices.

Remembered Highways

Angled somewhat north of west the roadway
bordering buildings on our seniors' campus
tracks four lanes through urban sprawl, narrowing
six miles out half way to the Andice T
where a short spur connects with a major
north-south highway bound for wooded rolling
hills and bare plains some miles farther on,
while restricted here by growing numbers
of virus cases, we former travelers
speculate outbound destinations
for younger families' well loaded vans.

Recollections

Do you still transcribe, boy, page after page,
register owners and number transactions?
You have titles for your numbering,
but you learned to count at this table
naming our dominoes by their dots.

You never bring your machines in here where
we know the tales, the timber we cut
and all the derricks we swung up, the big
wells that blew in and some sad dry holes.
Number those, boy, in your register.

Somewhat Independent Living

Confined mostly to our room we listen
for voices down the hall that predict
our noon meal, the delivery of mail,
perhaps a package we expected
two days ago with a pound of Peet's
we've lived without since Wednesday morning.

The exercise clique and the bridge club
no longer gather Tuesdays and Thursdays
and my Cardinals fan club meets online,
our conversations not much curtailed
by the absence of ball games this season
since Musial and Curt Flood dominate
our usual topics for argument
or Gibson and the sixty-eight collapse.

Delaying a Gift

Some of our children gave her the jigsaw
puzzle, an early gift that Christmas,
but she stood the box shrink wrapped on a shelf
to show books stacked spines out with bright title
lettering on colorful dust covers
where it stayed into January when,
unnoticed, she put the box out of sight.

Then, three weeks into Lent, she brought those
stacked spines and bright titles into view,
scattered the colored pieces across
our dining room table and began
to piece them together, drawing out
the process beyond our quieter Easter
toward hoped for release from isolation.

Watching Swallows

Is it too hard to recall yesterday's
slow climb through another uneventful
afternoon and sudden slip into dusk;
while I wonder what that day had hoped
to teach me with its routine practices,
swallows adorn the evening with swoops
and dives as they did the three or thirteen
before when you noticed peculiar patterns
repeated from day to day that I fail
to see as we wait out another Wednesday.

The Realization

Yesterday for breakfast we finished
what had seemed a more than generous supply
of our chosen cereals, even
mini wheat square dust I usually avoid
soaked up the last of our two percent milk.

We have bread for toast tomorrow
but used the last butter Tuesday morning.
Groceries, they say, will be delivered
perhaps Monday, by Wednesday they're sure.

She hands me yesterday's paper folded
to show lines of vehicles waiting
for food pantry pick up in the lot
behind shut down Southside Middle School,
below the fold, longer lines at the clinic.

Creation's Lament

If some Word somewhere uttered this world
into being it mispronounced itself.
Word may have stuttered or lost the grammar
of language and left creation unbalanced,
so we have swung 'round toward destruction,
lost touch with Word's still creating presence.

Creatures Word meant for cooperation
gather only for themselves, avoiding
common effort and shared resources,
walling up our gatherings against fear
of more equitable distribution
and Word's repeated revealing of our
careless acquisition, considered
exclusion and calculated accounting.

Distanced Ritual

Burial bells at St. Theresa's sound
out now familiar tones as the Sexton
and a younger priest complete essential
services for the small family gathered
in masks before the pall placed early
by bearers in the newly opened section
of the graveyard still without monuments.

We join these near daily rituals
from our third floor apartment balcony
across Laurel Avenue, willing
our participation known to mourners
who seldom lift their gaze from the path toward
cars left idling at the gate beneath us.

The Feast in a Strict Season

The faithful process with distant spacing
up the bare dirt road that divides the town
toward the church built atop its one ridge.
We walk behind the old priest and acolytes
with the crucifix and tarnished censer
swinging smoke that does not cloud our doubt.

We are an anxious remnant scattered
outside the church door to hear, in snatches,
the priest read early mass and watch him
pass cup and bread from table to his lips.

Leaving, a few smile greetings to friends
or lift a hand to those across the road.
Most return, heads bowed, to now somber
tables for their quieter Easter meal
and a thin edge of hope lighting the room.

Calculating the Damage

We drove out along the old road crumbling
over sand hills and clumps of Johnson grass
around occasional scrub Juniper
where we bought our first house together,
a few miles west of the Pine belt.

That place sits empty now, the back screen door
hanging loose from one rusted hinge, the windmill
fallen into the water tank, the barn
dismantled for reusable lumber.

The foundation seems solid, but the roof
has collapsed, and the porch no longer
connects to the house where two walls caved in.
Is anything left worth repair? you ask,
and I am unable to answer.

No Season for Silence

If you cannot keep dancing, never stop singing.
You hold the world together with your chorus.
Your notes and tones breathed in isolation
make our breathing possible. Your voices knit
together a framework for this fractured moment.

We no longer march with banners flying
but your strings and trumpets, ivory keys
and open lips dismantle structures restricting
any volume not of their own making.

A Grammar of Good Trouble
In memory of John R. Lewis

Have we grown comfortable with the language
of despair and the vocabulary
of hopelessness we have now learned to use?
Is the renewed grammar of what's possible
offering us a familiar structure
we're no longer prepared to employ?

How easily we have composed critique
and lined out the limits of actions
in our carefully patterned protest
against evils we so clearly describe.

Are we able to revise our despair
when confronted by terminologies
of hope and open arenas where
good grammar could lead to good deeds
and good deeds to trouble, good trouble?

In The Beginning

We will struggle to shore up shattered structures
of lives we thought overly demanding,
too many tasks and excess expectations
from friends and family and colleagues that seemed
too often to fill cherished spaces
we planned to keep empty for ourselves.

Empty has become our way of living
and we yearn to use again those habits
of cooperation and community
now atrophied where we set them aside
last March expecting a brief lockdown.
Perhaps we'll welcome new expectations,
tackle every task together and find
new habits in those shattered structures.

Milton Jordan has lived in the Southwest, the Northwest and the Midwest and worked as a newspaper reporter, sawmill lumber grader, social worker with teen-age boys, shovel wielder on archaeological projects, public school teacher and preacher. His essays, poems, reviews and stories have been published in anthologies and literary and popular journals. Milton is author or Editor of ten books. His most recent poetry collection, *What the Rivers Gather*, was published by Stephen F. Austin State University Press in 2020, and he edited the anthology *No Season for Silence: Texas Poets and Pandemic*, Kallisto Gaia Press, 2020. He is retired and lives in Georgetown, Texas, with the musician Anne Elton Jordan.

www.ingramcontent.com/pod-product-compliance
Lightning Source LLC
LaVergne TN
LVHW040117080426
835507LV00041B/1276